BLUE SHARKS

▲TAMMY KENNINGTON

Published in the United States of America by Cherry Lake Publishing
Ann Arbor, Michigan
www.cherrylakepublishing.com

Consultants: Dominique A. Didier, Associate Professor, Department of Biology, Millersville University;
Marla Conn, ReadAbility, Inc.
Editorial direction: Red Line Editorial
Book design and illustration: Sleeping Bear Press

Photo Credits: Dray van Beeck/Shutterstock Images, cover, 1, 11, 21; Sleeping Bear Press, 5; FAUP/
Shutterstock Images, 7; Shutterstock Images, 9; iStockphoto, 13; iStockphoto/Thinkstock, 15; Rich Carey/
Shutterstock Images, 17; Shane Gross/Shutterstock Images, 19, 22, 28; Jim Agronick/Shutterstock
Images, 25; Jessica L. Archibald/Shutterstock Images, 27

Library of Congress Cataloging-in-Publication Data
Kennington, Tammy.
  Blue sharks / Tammy Kennington.
      p. cm. — (Exploring our oceans)
  Audience: 008.
  Audience: Grades 4 to 6.
  Includes index.
  ISBN 978-1-62431-404-9 (hardcover) — ISBN 978-1-62431-480-3 (pbk.) — ISBN 978-1-62431-442-1 (pdf)
  — ISBN 978-1-62431-518-3 (ebook)
  1. Blue shark—Juvenile literature. I. Title.

  QL638.95.C3K46 2014
  597.3'4—dc23   2013006126

Cherry Lake Publishing would like to acknowledge the work of
The Partnership for 21st Century Skills. Please visit *www.p21.org*
for more information.

Printed in the United States of America
Corporate Graphics Inc.
July 2013
CLFA11

ABOUT THE AUTHOR

Tammy Kennington holds a bachelor of arts in elementary education and is a certified reading
intervention specialist. She currently serves as a preschool director. Tammy lives in Colorado
Springs, Colorado, with her husband and four children.

TABLE OF CONTENTS

CHAPTER 1
Easy to Identify 4

CHAPTER 2
An Unusual Blue 8

CHAPTER 3
Hunting and Eating 16

CHAPTER 4
From Pup to Predator 20

CHAPTER 5
Threats 24

THINK ABOUT IT 30

LEARN MORE 31

GLOSSARY 32

INDEX..32

Easy to Identify

The blue shark is one of the most common sharks in the world. Its sleek, jet-shaped body is easy to recognize. The blue shark is just one of about 400 other kinds of sharks in the world. It was first identified and named by Swedish scientist Carolus Linnaeus in 1758.

The blue shark is more curious than aggressive. Although this fish rarely attacks humans, it can be dangerous. Blue sharks can harm divers who may have food items, such as freshly killed fish, with them. Sometimes hungry blue sharks will charge a boat that is carrying a large catch of fish. People should treat any encounter with a blue shark with caution.

RANGE MAP

ARCTIC OCEAN

North America

Europe

Asia

ATLANTIC OCEAN

PACIFIC OCEAN

Africa

South America

INDIAN OCEAN

PACIFIC OCEAN

Australia

☐ RANGE OF BLUE SHARK

Blue sharks avoid the colder waters around the poles.

Blue sharks have a wide range. They live in all tropical and **temperate** seas. The sharks live in oceans from Newfoundland to Argentina and from Norway to South Africa. They prefer to swim in mild or cool tropical waters. Blue sharks are **pelagic**. This means they are mostly found near the surface of deep, open waters. They can also swim or dive to as deep as about 1,100 feet (335 m) below the surface. Blue sharks rarely swim close to shore.

Blue sharks often **migrate** to follow warmer waters. Blue sharks in the Pacific Ocean migrate north in the summer and south in the winter. In the Atlantic Ocean, blue sharks follow the ocean currents to migrate from the United States to Europe. Other blue sharks migrate from northern Africa to the northern Caribbean. Some blue sharks have traveled more than 3,000 miles (4,828 km). This would be like traveling from California to Maine. ◢

Blue sharks are easily recognized in the ocean.

LOOK AGAIN

LOOK AT THIS IMAGE CLOSELY. WHAT IS SOMETHING THAT SURPRISES YOU ABOUT THE BLUE SHARK?

CHAPTER 2

An Unusual Blue

The blue shark has a unique look. It has a slender body and a cone-shaped snout. This sleek shape allows the shark to move smoothly and swiftly through the water. The blue shark has long pectoral fins on the sides of its body. It has large eyes on the sides of its head. The average blue shark is about 7 to 11 feet (2.1–3.4 m) long. It weighs about 500 pounds (227 kg). This is almost the weight of three average adult men.

Most sharks are gray. The blue shark is dark blue. Its belly is white. This coloring is called **countershading**.

Countershading lets the shark blend in to its surroundings. Seen from above, the shark's blue top blends in with the darker ocean water beneath it. When seen from below, the shark's white belly looks similar to the lighter-colored water of the surface.

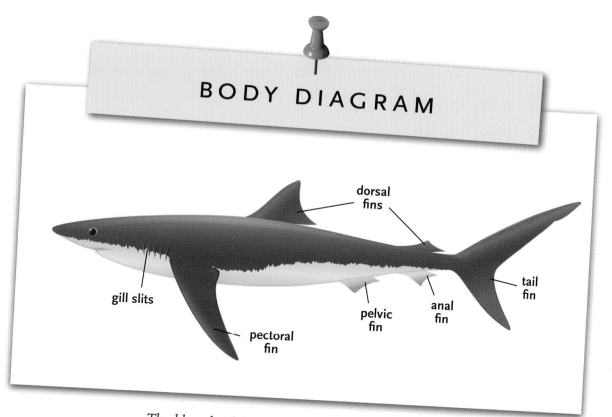

BODY DIAGRAM

dorsal fins

gill slits

pectoral fin

pelvic fin

anal fin

tail fin

The blue shark has a unique body shape and color.

The blue shark's skeleton is made of **cartilage.**
Cartilage is the stiff, flexible material that all shark
skeletons are made of. It is less dense than bone. This
makes the shark lighter in the water than if it had a
skeleton made of bone, as other fish have. Cartilage is
also durable. Think of a human ear. It is made of cartilage
and can bend without breaking. Cartilage is also springy.
It gives the shark more flexibility for swimming and
turning quickly.

The blue shark's skin is made of millions of tiny
dermal denticles. Dermal denticles are rigid, tooth-
shaped plates. They provide protection from both predators
and parasites. They have been compared to armor worn
by knights for protection. Dermal denticles are almost
invisible to the naked eye. They are closely arranged and
point toward the tail. They feel like sandpaper when
rubbed against the grain. In fact, people have used the
blue shark's skin as a type of sandpaper.

A white belly helps a blue shark blend in with its surroundings and sneak up on prey.

LOOK AGAIN

Look closely at this photo. What stands out to you? What information can you gather from the photo that you could not learn from the text?

Each species of shark has a different type and arrangement of dermal denticles. The blue shark's dermal denticles are close together along the snout and fins. This tight arrangement makes a very smooth surface. Olympic swimmers wear sleek tight suits to make their skin smooth so they can swim faster. The blue shark has something similar. Its smooth skin allows it to have quick bursts of speed when it swims. Female blue sharks have skin three times thicker than the skin of males. Thicker skin protects the females from being injured if the males bite them when the sharks **mate**.

The blue shark's teeth are in a tooth bed. The tooth bed shifts new teeth forward when teeth need to be replaced. Each tooth is replaced every eight to 15 days. The blue shark has almost 60 **serrated** teeth in three rows. A blue shark can take a bite out of nearly any animal it chooses. Its teeth easily cut through the skin and break the bones of its prey.

The blue shark's sleek body helps it swim quickly in the water.

The blue shark belongs to a family of sharks known for having differently shaped upper and lower teeth. It has broad, curved upper teeth and straight, slender lower teeth. Both types of teeth allow the blue shark to easily grasp small prey and to attack larger food sources, such as other sharks or dead whales. The teeth work together like a fork and a knife. One set of teeth grips the prey. The other set slices the prey.

The blue shark has five gill slits on each side of its head. Inside the gill slits are gills. As the shark swims, water enters the shark's mouth and passes over the gills. The gills are tissues that contain lots of small blood vessels called capillaries. When water flows over the tissue, oxygen from the water enters into these capillaries. The bloodstream carries the oxygen throughout the shark's body. Water exits the shark through the gill slits.

The blue shark also has gill rakers on its gills. Gill rakers are not involved in breathing. Scientists think gill rakers help protect the gills from objects in the water that

The water that a blue shark takes in to breathe leaves the body through gill slits near the pectoral fin.

may harm them. They may also keep squid from slipping away or help blue sharks eat plankton.

The blue shark has a **retractable** third eyelid. The third eyelid is a flap of skin the blue shark rotates over its eye when it attacks prey or during threatening situations. This feature, shared with other types of sharks, allows the blue shark to protect its vision. But protecting its vision causes momentary blindness for the blue shark. ◢

CHAPTER 3

HUNTING AND EATING

The blue shark is a **carnivore**. It eats all day, but it is more active at night. The blue shark eats bony fish like mackerel, tuna, and sardines. It also eats shrimp and squid. The blue shark has even been known to eat seabirds, dead seals, and smaller sharks. The blue shark has a big appetite. Sometimes it will eat so much food it throws up. Then it will eat some more.

Blue sharks like to cruise slowly through large schools of fish. This allows the blue shark to use less energy than swimming quickly. It can swim swiftly

to catch its prey if needed. Blue sharks are among the
fastest sharks when it comes to quick bursts of swimming.

*A blue shark may swim through a school of
mackerel to catch as much prey as possible.*

The blue shark uses **electroreception** to help it find prey. Electroreception is known as the shark's sixth sense. Thousands of small pores are located on the shark's snout and jaw. These pores are filled with a gel-like substance. The substance passes on electrical currents in the water to cells that detect electrical currents. Every living creature sends out electrical currents. For example, every time a person flexes a muscle or even blinks, he or she is sending out a very tiny electrical signal. Humans can't detect these signals, but sharks can. They have specialized brains that let them detect these electrical signals. A shark can detect the electrical signals of a creature swimming nearby. This is one way it locates prey.

Blue sharks often hunt in groups. They have been called the "wolves of the sea." They gather to feed on schools of anchovies. They have also been seen behind fishing boats loaded with full nets of fish. Blue sharks hunt alone too. Once they find their prey, they often circle it and then attack. Squid are possibly the blue shark's favorite prey. Squid are an easy meal because they often form large groups.

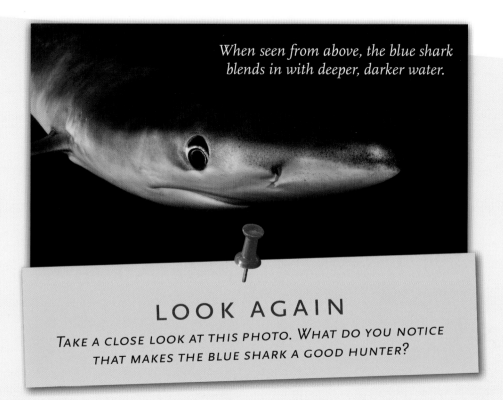

When seen from above, the blue shark blends in with deeper, darker water.

LOOK AGAIN

TAKE A CLOSE LOOK AT THIS PHOTO. WHAT DO YOU NOTICE THAT MAKES THE BLUE SHARK A GOOD HUNTER?

The blue shark takes advantage of weak, sick, or dying whales and porpoises. This feeding habit serves an important role. It improves the overall health of creatures in the ocean. ◀

CHAPTER 4

From Pup to Predator

After mating, a female blue shark is pregnant for nine to 12 months. The mother travels to a special place called a nursery to give birth. One known nursery is off the coast of Brazil. Blue sharks have large families. A mother gives birth to an average litter of 25 to 50 live **pups**. Depending on her size, a mother may have as few as four and as many as 135 babies. The number of male and female pups in each litter is usually about even.

A mother blue shark travels to a nursery so her young can be born in a safe place.

Male and female blue sharks reach maturity at ages four to six.

Blue sharks begin life as small as human infants—between 16 and 20 inches (40.6–50.8 cm) long. The pups swim away from their mothers as soon as they are born. This may be to avoid getting eaten by their mothers or other shark predators. The pups must fend for themselves right away. Instinctively, they know how to hunt and defend themselves from predators.

Blue sharks separate into groups made up of males and females when they are juveniles. When they are about five years old they separate from the juvenile groups and join all-male or all-female groups of adults. Some scientists believe they do this because sharks that are close to the same size gather in the same feeding areas.

Both male and female sharks reach maturity at four to six years old. Average adult blue sharks are about 6 to 7 feet (1.8–2.1 m) long. They can be as long as 13 feet (4 m). ◢

GO DEEPER

AFTER READING THIS CHAPTER CLOSELY,
SUMMARIZE THE LIFE CYCLE OF A BLUE SHARK.

CHAPTER 5

THREATS

The blue shark is near the top of the food chain. It has only a few natural predators. These predators include the California sea lion and larger sharks. The shortfin mako and the great white shark are heavier and faster than the blue shark. They can target the blue shark as prey.

Some of the blue shark's smallest enemies are parasites. The parasites usually get into the shark's body when the shark eats infected prey. The blue shark is known to host up to 3,000 parasites. The shark serves as a home and food source for these creatures. One of the most common

Blue sharks can be prey for great white sharks.

parasites is the tapeworm. It lives in the shark's digestive system and feasts on the food the shark eats. The tapeworm is more of a nuisance than a health threat.

Other small animals are dangerous to the shark. Copepods live in the blue shark's nose and gills and on the fins. Some of these copepods feed on the shark's mucous, skin, or blood. These creatures become dangerous to the blue shark when they affect its eyesight and gill function. Without good vision, a blue shark is vulnerable to attack. Once its gills no longer work, the shark will die.

Fishing is the greatest threat to the blue shark's survival. Every year, about 10 to 20 million blue sharks are killed. They are either fished for sport or caught accidentally by fishermen catching mackerel, salmon, or other fish. The blue shark's meat is only edible for a short time after it has been caught. Sport fishermen often remove the blue shark's fins. The fins are sold at a high price to people who make shark fin soup. This soup is a popular dish in many Asian countries.

Blue sharks can get caught in nets that are meant for other fish.

*Researchers continue to study blue
sharks to learn ways to protect them.*

The International Union for the Conservation of Nature (IUCN) lists blue sharks as Near Threatened on their Red List of Threatened Species. This means the population is not yet in great trouble. Conservation groups such as the IUCN and the International Commission for the Conservation of Atlantic Tunas (ICCAT) watch blue sharks to make sure they do not become more threatened. These groups say more needs to be done by many countries to prevent the blue shark from becoming an endangered species. ◢

THINK ABOUT IT

EXPLAIN HOW THE AUTHOR PROVIDES EVIDENCE OF THE BLUE SHARK'S THREATENED STATUS AROUND THE WORLD.

THINK ABOUT IT

▲ What is the most interesting fact you learned about blue sharks? What else would you like to know? Visit the library and choose another book about blue sharks. How does the information compare to what you have already learned?

▲ Read Chapter 2 again. Compare the similarities and contrast the differences of sharks and bony fish. What do you think is the blue shark's most unique trait?

▲ Review Chapter 3. What is the main idea? Choose two or three details that support the main idea.

▲ In Chapter 5, you learned the blue shark is listed as a Near Threatened species. Do you think it is important to protect the blue shark? Why or why not?

LEARN MORE

FURTHER READING

MacQuitty, Miranda. *Shark*. New York: DK, 2011.

Marsico, Katie. *Sharks*. New York: Scholastic, 2011.

Musgrave, Ruth. *Everything Sharks*. Washington, DC: National Geographic, 2011.

Parker, Steve. *100 Facts on Sharks*. Thaxted, UK: Miles Kelly, 2010.

WEB SITES

Discovery Kids—Sharks
http://kids.discovery.com/gaming/shark-week

This Web site lets readers learn about shark attack survivals and play games.

National Geographic—Sharks
http://animals.nationalgeographic.com/animals/sharks

Readers discover different species of sharks, learn more about the ocean, and play games at this Web site.

GLOSSARY

carnivore (KAR-nuh-vor) an animal that eats meat

cartilage (KAHR-tuh-lij) a hard, flexible tissue that forms certain parts of animals' bodies, such as a human ear or a shark's skeleton

countershading (KOUN-tur-shay-ding) the light and dark coloring of an animal to help it blend into its surroundings

dermal denticle (DUR-mul DEN-ti-kuhl) a sharp, tooth-like piece, such as the scale of a shark

electroreception (i-lek-tro-ri-SEP-shuhn) a type of sense that allows sharks to detect the heartbeats of their prey

mate (MATE) to join together to produce babies

migrate (MYE-grate) to move from one area to another

pelagic (puh-LAY-jik) living in open waters

pup (PUP) a baby shark

retractable (ri-TRAK-tuh-bul) able to be pulled back in

serrated (SER-ay-tid) looking like the blade of a saw

temperate (TEM-pur-it) not extremely hot or cold

INDEX

birth, 20
body shape, 4
breathing, 14

conservation, 29
countershading, 8–9

habitat, 6
hunting, 16–17, 18–19

juvenile, 23

migrate, 6

physical features, 8–10, 12, 14–15
prey, 12, 14, 15, 16–17, 18–19, 24
pup, 20, 22

size, 8, 20, 22, 23

teeth, 12, 14
threats, human, 26
threats, natural, 24, 26